T.I.M.E. for Success

102 Quotes to Teach, Inspire, Motivate, and Empower

By Dr. Robert Jones, MNLP, MHt, MTT
and Brenda Jones, MA, MNLP, MHt, MTT
www.integrateTIME.com
www.lavenderandTIME.com

T.I.M.E. for Success
102 Quotes to Teach, Inspire, Motivate, and Empower

By Dr. Robert Jones, MNLP, MHt, MTT and Brenda Jones, MA, MNLP, MHt, MTT

Printed by CreateSpace
Published by Brenda Jones, Robert Jones, and Integrate TIME
www.integrateTIME.com

ISBN: 0-9985537-0-0
ISBN-13: 978-0-9985537-0-2

Printed in the United States of America
10 9 8 7 6 5 4 3 2 1

Dedicated to A and A, our sweet, beautiful girls, who teach, inspire, motivate, and empower us daily.

You are the reasons we do what we do and why we strive to share our message with others. We love you to the moon and back!

"May all your dreams stay big" ~Rascal Flatts

Introduction

Designed to stimulate the growth or development of daily self-motivation to help you achieve your goals and dreams, "TIME for Success" is packed with quotes that will *teach, inspire, motivate, and empower* you daily!

What you think is what you become, so take a break from the challenges and busy-ness of daily life to prepare yourself to take on the day and to reflect on your successes by recording your experiences as you move through each quote.

How to use this book:
Before you begin your day, open to a quote, either in order or at random (you choose!), read it aloud to yourself, think of what that quote means to you, and complete the Prep TIME journal prompts. You may wish to take a picture of the quote and store it in your phone or write it on a sticky note as a reminder throughout the day. Before bed, complete the Review TIME journal prompts.

Let this book tell your story through your eyes.

It's your *TIME for Success*, so express yourself!

"As a single footstep will not make a path on the earth, so a single thought will not make a pathway in the mind. To make a deep physical path, we walk again and again. To make a deep mental path, we must think over and over the kind of thoughts we wish to dominate our lives. " ~Henry David Thoreau

Prep TIME
I am applying this quote today by:

_____
_____
_____

I can share this quote with:

_____
_____
_____

Review TIME
I applied this quote today by:

_____
_____
_____

Moving forward I can:

_____
_____
_____

"A goal without a date is just a dream."
~Milton H. Erickson

Prep TIME
I am applying this quote today by:

_____
_____
_____

I can share this quote with:

_____
_____
_____

Review TIME
I applied this quote today by:

_____
_____
_____

Moving forward I can:

_____
_____
_____

"My happiness grows in direct proportion to my acceptance, and in inverse proportion to my expectations." ~Michael J. Fox

Prep TIME
I am applying this quote today by:

_____
_____
_____

I can share this quote with:

_____
_____
_____

Review TIME
I applied this quote today by:

_____
_____
_____

Moving forward I can:

_____
_____
_____

"All our dreams can come true, if we have the courage to pursue them." ~Walt Disney

Prep TIME
I am applying this quote today by:

_____
_____
_____

I can share this quote with:

_____
_____
_____

Review TIME
I applied this quote today by:

_____
_____
_____

Moving forward I can:

_____
_____
_____

"Big changes can sometimes be difficult and downright scary. Make small ones and watch them add up." ~Brenda Jones

Prep TIME
I am applying this quote today by:

_____
_____
_____

I can share this quote with:

_____
_____
_____

Review TIME
I applied this quote today by:

_____
_____
_____

Moving forward I can:

_____
_____
_____

"When saying 'yes' to others, make sure you aren't saying 'no' to yourself." ~Paulo Coehlo

Prep TIME
I am applying this quote today by:

_____
_____
_____

I can share this quote with:

_____
_____
_____

Review TIME
I applied this quote today by:

_____
_____
_____

Moving forward I can:

_____
_____
_____

"Success is getting what you want. Happiness is wanting what you get." ~Dale Carnegie

Prep TIME
I am applying this quote today by:

_____
_____
_____

I can share this quote with:

_____
_____
_____

Review TIME
I applied this quote today by:

_____
_____
_____

Moving forward I can:

_____
_____
_____

"It does not matter how slowly you go as long as you do not stop." ~Confucius

Prep TIME
I am applying this quote today by:

_____

_____

_____

I can share this quote with:

_____

_____

_____

Review TIME
I applied this quote today by:

_____

_____

_____

Moving forward I can:

_____

_____

_____

"We can't help everyone, but everyone can help someone." ~Ronald Reagan

Prep TIME
I am applying this quote today by:

_____
_____
_____

I can share this quote with:

_____
_____
_____

Review TIME
I applied this quote today by:

_____
_____
_____

Moving forward I can:

_____
_____
_____

**"If you really want to do something, you will find a way. If you don't, you'll find an excuse."
~Jim Rohn**

Prep TIME
I am applying this quote today by:

_____
_____
_____

I can share this quote with:

_____
_____
_____

Review TIME
I applied this quote today by:

_____
_____
_____

Moving forward I can:

_____
_____
_____

"If they can't learn the way we teach, we teach the way they learn." Ole Ivar Lovaas

Prep TIME
I am applying this quote today by:

_____
_____
_____

I can share this quote with:

_____
_____
_____

Review TIME
I applied this quote today by:

_____
_____
_____

Moving forward I can:

_____
_____
_____

"In essence, if we want to direct our lives, we must take control of our consistent actions. It's not what we do once in a while that shapes our lives, but what we do consistently."
~Tony Robbins

Prep TIME
I am applying this quote today by:

_____
_____
_____

I can share this quote with:

_____
_____
_____

Review TIME
I applied this quote today by:

_____
_____
_____

Moving forward I can:

_____
_____
_____

"Tell me and I forget. Teach me and I remember. Involve me and I learn." ~Benjamin Franklin

Prep TIME
I am applying this quote today by:

_____
_____
_____

I can share this quote with:

_____
_____
_____

Review TIME
I applied this quote today by:

_____
_____
_____

Moving forward I can:

_____
_____
_____

"If you accept the expectations of others, especially negative ones, then you never will change the outcome." ~Michael Jordan

Prep TIME
I am applying this quote today by:

_____
_____
_____

I can share this quote with:

_____
_____
_____

Review TIME
I applied this quote today by:

_____
_____
_____

Moving forward I can:

_____
_____
_____

"Try to love someone who you want to hate, because they are just like you, somewhere inside, in a way you may never expect, in a way that resounds so deeply within you that you cannot believe it." ~Margaret Cho

Prep TIME
I am applying this quote today by:

_____
_____
_____

I can share this quote with:

_____
_____
_____

Review TIME
I applied this quote today by:

_____
_____
_____

Moving forward I can:

_____
_____
_____

"The beginning is the most important part of the work." ~Plato

Prep TIME
I am applying this quote today by:

_____
_____
_____

I can share this quote with:

_____
_____
_____

Review TIME
I applied this quote today by:

_____
_____
_____

Moving forward I can:

_____
_____
_____

"I don't want to say everything happens for a reason but every day is lined up right next to the other one for a reason. The best you can do is do each day well with kindness and as a good person." ~Mayim Bialik

Prep TIME
I am applying this quote today by:

_____
_____
_____

I can share this quote with:

_____
_____
_____

Review TIME
I applied this quote today by:

_____
_____
_____

Moving forward I can:

_____
_____
_____

"I have learned over the years that when one's mind is made up, that diminishes fear; knowing what must be done does away with fear." ~Rosa Parks

Prep TIME
I am applying this quote today by:

_____
_____
_____

I can share this quote with:

_____
_____
_____

Review TIME
I applied this quote today by:

_____
_____
_____

Moving forward I can:

_____
_____
_____

"Look up at the stars and not down at your feet. Try to make sense of what you see, and wonder about what makes the universe exist. Be curious." ~Stephen Hawking

Prep TIME
I am applying this quote today by:

_____

_____

_____

I can share this quote with:

_____

_____

_____

Review TIME
I applied this quote today by:

_____

_____

_____

Moving forward I can:

_____

_____

_____

"If you aren't in the moment, you are either looking forward to uncertainty, or back to pain and regret." ~Jim Carrey

Prep TIME
I am applying this quote today by:

_____
_____
_____

I can share this quote with:

_____
_____
_____

Review TIME
I applied this quote today by:

_____
_____
_____

Moving forward I can:

_____
_____
_____

"Believe in love. Believe in magic. Hell, believe in Santa Claus. Believe in others. Believe in yourself. Believe in your dreams. If you don't, who will?" ~Jon Bon Jovi

Prep TIME
I am applying this quote today by:
_____
_____
_____

I can share this quote with:
_____
_____
_____

Review TIME
I applied this quote today by:
_____
_____
_____

Moving forward I can:
_____
_____
_____

"Your journey has molded you for your greater good, and it was exactly what it needed to be. Don't think that you've lost time. It took each and every situation you have encountered to bring you to the now. And now is right on time." ~Asha Tyson

Prep TIME
I am applying this quote today by:

_____
_____
_____

I can share this quote with:

_____
_____
_____

Review TIME
I applied this quote today by:

_____
_____
_____

Moving forward I can:

_____
_____
_____

"If you don't like something, change it. If you can't change it, change your attitude."
~Maya Angelou

Prep TIME
I am applying this quote today by:

_____

_____

_____

I can share this quote with:

_____

_____

_____

Review TIME
I applied this quote today by:

_____

_____

_____

Moving forward I can:

_____

_____

_____

"If your inner life is not producing what you would like on the outside, don't be discouraged... just be willing to change."
~Joyce Meyer

Prep TIME
I am applying this quote today by:
_____
_____
_____

I can share this quote with:
_____
_____
_____

Review TIME
I applied this quote today by:
_____
_____
_____

Moving forward I can:
_____
_____
_____

"Problems are simply opportunities viewed through negative filters." ~Brenda Jones

Prep TIME
I am applying this quote today by:

_____
_____
_____

I can share this quote with:

_____
_____
_____

Review TIME
I applied this quote today by:

_____
_____
_____

Moving forward I can:

_____
_____
_____

"Success is not final, failure is not fatal; it is courage to continue that counts."
~Winston Churchill

Prep TIME
I am applying this quote today by:

_____
_____
_____

I can share this quote with:

_____
_____
_____

Review TIME
I applied this quote today by:

_____
_____
_____

Moving forward I can:

_____
_____
_____

"Progress is impossible without change, and those who cannot change their minds cannot change anything." ~George Bernard Shaw

Prep TIME
I am applying this quote today by:

_____
_____
_____

I can share this quote with:

_____
_____
_____

Review TIME
I applied this quote today by:

_____
_____
_____

Moving forward I can:

_____
_____
_____

"**Promise me you'll always remember: You're braver than you believe, and stronger than you seem, and smarter than you think.**"
~A. A. Milne

Prep TIME
I am applying this quote today by:

_____
_____
_____

I can share this quote with:

_____
_____
_____

Review TIME
I applied this quote today by:

_____
_____
_____

Moving forward I can:

_____
_____
_____

"Believe you can and you're halfway there."
~Theodore Roosevelt

Prep TIME
I am applying this quote today by:

_____
_____
_____

I can share this quote with:

_____
_____
_____

Review TIME
I applied this quote today by:

_____
_____
_____

Moving forward I can:

_____
_____
_____

"If it wasn't hard, everyone would do it. It's the hard that makes it great." ~Tom Hanks

Prep TIME
I am applying this quote today by:

_____
_____
_____

I can share this quote with:

_____
_____
_____

Review TIME
I applied this quote today by:

_____
_____
_____

Moving forward I can:

_____
_____
_____

"If your actions inspire others to dream more, learn more, do more and become more, you are a leader." ~John Quincy Adams

Prep TIME
I am applying this quote today by:

_____
_____
_____

I can share this quote with:

_____
_____
_____

Review TIME
I applied this quote today by:

_____
_____
_____

Moving forward I can:

_____
_____
_____

"There is little success where there is little laughter." ~Andrew Carnegie

Prep TIME
I am applying this quote today by:

_____
_____
_____

I can share this quote with:

_____
_____
_____

Review TIME
I applied this quote today by:

_____
_____
_____

Moving forward I can:

_____
_____
_____

"Today I shall behave, as if this is the day I will be remembered." ~Dr. Seuss

Prep TIME
I am applying this quote today by:

_____
_____
_____

I can share this quote with:

_____
_____
_____

Review TIME
I applied this quote today by:

_____
_____
_____

Moving forward I can:

_____
_____
_____

"No matter what people tell you, words and ideas can change the world." ~Robin Williams

Prep TIME
I am applying this quote today by:

_____
_____
_____

I can share this quote with:

_____
_____
_____

Review TIME
I applied this quote today by:

_____
_____
_____

Moving forward I can:

_____
_____
_____

"The key to success is to focus our conscious mind on things we desire not things we fear."
~Brian Tracy

Prep TIME
I am applying this quote today by:

_____
_____
_____

I can share this quote with:

_____
_____
_____

Review TIME
I applied this quote today by:

_____
_____
_____

Moving forward I can:

_____
_____
_____

"You should tell yourself frequently 'I will only react to constructive suggestions.' This gives you positive ammunition against your own negative thoughts and those of others."
~Jane Roberts

Prep TIME
I am applying this quote today by:

_____
_____
_____

I can share this quote with:

_____
_____
_____

Review TIME
I applied this quote today by:

_____
_____
_____

Moving forward I can:

_____
_____
_____

"Courage is not the absence of fear but rather the judgement that something is more important than fear; The brave may not live forever but the cautious do not live at all."
~Meg Cabot

Prep TIME
I am applying this quote today by:

_____
_____
_____

I can share this quote with:

_____
_____
_____

Review TIME
I applied this quote today by:

_____
_____
_____

Moving forward I can:

_____
_____
_____

"Optimism is the faith that leads to achievement. Nothing can be done without hope and confidence." ~Helen Keller

Prep TIME
I am applying this quote today by:

_____
_____
_____

I can share this quote with:

_____
_____
_____

Review TIME
I applied this quote today by:

_____
_____
_____

Moving forward I can:

_____
_____
_____

"Smile in the mirror. Do that every morning and you'll start to see a big difference in your life." ~Yoko Ono

Prep TIME
I am applying this quote today by:

_____
_____
_____

I can share this quote with:

_____
_____
_____

Review TIME
I applied this quote today by:

_____
_____
_____

Moving forward I can:

_____
_____
_____

"Some failure in life is inevitable. It is impossible to live without failing at something, unless you live so cautiously that you might as well not have lived at all — in which case, you fail by default."
~J. K. Rowling

Prep TIME
I am applying this quote today by:

_____
_____
_____

I can share this quote with:

_____
_____
_____

Review TIME
I applied this quote today by:

_____
_____
_____

Moving forward I can:

_____
_____
_____

"The future belongs to those who believe in the beauty of their dreams."
~Eleanor Roosevelt

Prep TIME
I am applying this quote today by:

_____
_____
_____

I can share this quote with:

_____
_____
_____

Review TIME
I applied this quote today by:

_____
_____
_____

Moving forward I can:

_____
_____
_____

"As long as you're learning, there is no such thing as failure." ~Dr. Robert Jones

Prep TIME
I am applying this quote today by:

_____

_____

_____

I can share this quote with:

_____

_____

_____

Review TIME
I applied this quote today by:

_____

_____

_____

Moving forward I can:

_____

_____

_____

"If we did all the things we are capable of, we would literally astound ourselves."
~Thomas A. Edison

Prep TIME
I am applying this quote today by:

_____
_____
_____

I can share this quote with:

_____
_____
_____

Review TIME
I applied this quote today by:

_____
_____
_____

Moving forward I can:

_____
_____
_____

"In every day, there are 1,440 minutes. That means we have 1,440 daily opportunities to make a positive impact." ~Les Brown

Prep TIME
I am applying this quote today by:
_____
_____
_____

I can share this quote with:
_____
_____
_____

Review TIME
I applied this quote today by:
_____
_____
_____

Moving forward I can:
_____
_____
_____

"Listen to the mustn'ts, child. Listen to the don'ts. Listen to the shouldn'ts, the impossibles, the won'ts. Listen to the never haves, THEN listen close to me? Anything can happen, child. Anything can be."
~Shel Silverstein

Prep TIME
I am applying this quote today by:

_____
_____
_____

I can share this quote with:

_____
_____
_____

Review TIME
I applied this quote today by:

_____
_____
_____

Moving forward I can:

_____
_____
_____

"If we are not a little bit uncomfortable every day, we're not growing. All the good stuff is outside our comfort zone." ~Jack Canfield

Prep TIME
I am applying this quote today by:

_____
_____
_____

I can share this quote with:

_____
_____
_____

Review TIME
I applied this quote today by:

_____
_____
_____

Moving forward I can:

_____
_____
_____

"Carry out a random act of kindness, with no expectation of reward, safe in the knowledge that one day someone might do the same for you." ~Princess Diana

Prep TIME
I am applying this quote today by:

_____
_____
_____

I can share this quote with:

_____
_____
_____

Review TIME
I applied this quote today by:

_____
_____
_____

Moving forward I can:

_____
_____
_____

"A failure is not always a mistake, it may simply be the best one can do under the circumstances. The real mistake is to stop trying." ~B. F. Skinner

Prep TIME
I am applying this quote today by:

_____
_____
_____

I can share this quote with:

_____
_____
_____

Review TIME
I applied this quote today by:

_____
_____
_____

Moving forward I can:

_____
_____
_____

"Confidence isn't optimism or pessimism, and it's not a character attribute. It's the expectation of a positive outcome."
~Rosabeth Moss Kanter

Prep TIME
I am applying this quote today by:

_____
_____
_____

I can share this quote with:

_____
_____
_____

Review TIME
I applied this quote today by:

_____
_____
_____

Moving forward I can:

_____
_____
_____

"Find out who you are and do it on purpose."
~Dolly Parton

Prep TIME
I am applying this quote today by:

_____

_____

_____

I can share this quote with:

_____

_____

_____

Review TIME
I applied this quote today by:

_____

_____

_____

Moving forward I can:

_____

_____

_____

"A life lived in fear is a life half lived."
~Baz Luhrmann

Prep TIME
I am applying this quote today by:

_____

_____

_____

I can share this quote with:

_____

_____

_____

Review TIME
I applied this quote today by:

_____

_____

_____

Moving forward I can:

_____

_____

_____

"You're going to go through tough times - that's life. But I say, 'Nothing happens to you, it happens for you.' See the positive in negative events." ~Joel Osteen

Prep TIME
I am applying this quote today by:

_____
_____
_____

I can share this quote with:

_____
_____
_____

Review TIME
I applied this quote today by:

_____
_____
_____

Moving forward I can:

_____
_____
_____

"Visualize this thing that you want, see it, feel it, believe in it. Make your mental blue print, and begin to build." ~Robert Collier

Prep TIME
I am applying this quote today by:

_____
_____
_____

I can share this quote with:

_____
_____
_____

Review TIME
I applied this quote today by:

_____
_____
_____

Moving forward I can:

_____
_____
_____

"When people meet you, do you want them to be glad or sad? It's all up to you, Honey." ~Janet Zimmer

Prep TIME
I am applying this quote today by:

_____

_____

_____

I can share this quote with:

_____

_____

_____

Review TIME
I applied this quote today by:

_____

_____

_____

Moving forward I can:

_____

_____

_____

"Don't worry that children never listen to you; worry that they are always watching you." ~Robert Fulghum

Prep TIME
I am applying this quote today by:

_____
_____
_____

I can share this quote with:

_____
_____
_____

Review TIME
I applied this quote today by:

_____
_____
_____

Moving forward I can:

_____
_____
_____

"Failure is simply the opportunity to begin again, this time more intelligently."
~Henry Ford

Prep TIME
I am applying this quote today by:

_____

_____

_____

I can share this quote with:

_____

_____

_____

Review TIME
I applied this quote today by:

_____

_____

_____

Moving forward I can:

_____

_____

_____

"What you get by achieving your goals is not as important as what you become by achieving your goals." ~Zig Ziglar

Prep TIME
I am applying this quote today by:

_____
_____
_____

I can share this quote with:

_____
_____
_____

Review TIME
I applied this quote today by:

_____
_____
_____

Moving forward I can:

_____
_____
_____

"**You are the sum total of everything you've ever seen, heard, eaten, smelled, been told, forgot - it's all there. Everything influences each of us, and because of that I try to make sure that my experiences are positive."**
~Maya Angelou

Prep TIME
I am applying this quote today by:

_____
_____
_____

I can share this quote with:

_____
_____
_____

Review TIME
I applied this quote today by:

_____
_____
_____

Moving forward I can:

_____
_____
_____

"I attribute my success to this: I never gave or took any excuse." ~Florence Nightingale

Prep TIME
I am applying this quote today by:

_____
_____
_____

I can share this quote with:

_____
_____
_____

Review TIME
I applied this quote today by:

_____
_____
_____

Moving forward I can:

_____
_____
_____

"Success is a journey, not a destination. The doing is often more important than the outcome." ~Arthur Ashe

Prep TIME
I am applying this quote today by:

_____
_____
_____

I can share this quote with:

_____
_____
_____

Review TIME
I applied this quote today by:

_____
_____
_____

Moving forward I can:

_____
_____
_____

"Words are, in my not-so-humble opinion, our most inexhaustible source of magic. Capable of both inflicting injury, and remedying it."
~J. K. Rowling

Prep TIME
I am applying this quote today by:
_____
_____
_____

I can share this quote with:
_____
_____
_____

Review TIME
I applied this quote today by:
_____
_____
_____

Moving forward I can:
_____
_____
_____

"**Love yourself first and everything else falls into line. You really have to love yourself to get anything done in this world.**" ~Lucille Ball

Prep TIME
I am applying this quote today by:

_____
_____
_____

I can share this quote with:

_____
_____
_____

Review TIME
I applied this quote today by:

_____
_____
_____

Moving forward I can:

_____
_____
_____

"Life is not a bowl of cherries. Into each life some rain must fall. But if no rain, there would be no cherries." ~John Gardner

Prep TIME
I am applying this quote today by:

_____
_____
_____

I can share this quote with:

_____
_____
_____

Review TIME
I applied this quote today by:

_____
_____
_____

Moving forward I can:

_____
_____
_____

"Never mistake motion for action."
~Ernest Hemingway

Prep TIME
I am applying this quote today by:

_____
_____
_____

I can share this quote with:

_____
_____
_____

Review TIME
I applied this quote today by:

_____
_____
_____

Moving forward I can:

_____
_____
_____

"Problems are not stop signs, they are guidelines." ~Robert H. Schuller

Prep TIME
I am applying this quote today by:

_____
_____
_____

I can share this quote with:

_____
_____
_____

Review TIME
I applied this quote today by:

_____
_____
_____

Moving forward I can:

_____
_____
_____

"Follow your bliss and the universe will open
doors where there were only walls."
~Joseph Campbell

Prep TIME
I am applying this quote today by:
_____
_____
_____

I can share this quote with:
_____
_____
_____

Review TIME
I applied this quote today by:
_____
_____
_____

Moving forward I can:
_____
_____
_____

"Whether you think you can, or you think you can't -- you're right." ~Henry Ford

Prep TIME
I am applying this quote today by:

_____

_____

_____

I can share this quote with:

_____

_____

_____

Review TIME
I applied this quote today by:

_____

_____

_____

Moving forward I can:

_____

_____

_____

"Be strong, be fearless, be beautiful. And believe that anything is possible when you have the right people there to support you."
~Misty Copeland

Prep TIME
I am applying this quote today by:

_____
_____
_____

I can share this quote with:

_____
_____
_____

Review TIME
I applied this quote today by:

_____
_____
_____

Moving forward I can:

_____
_____
_____

"Integrity is everything. With it, you can weather all storms. Without it, even little things will derail you. Hold true to your commitments because relationships are either built or undone by them." ~Michael Stevenson

Prep TIME
I am applying this quote today by:

_____
_____
_____

I can share this quote with:

_____
_____
_____

Review TIME
I applied this quote today by:

_____
_____
_____

Moving forward I can:

_____
_____
_____

"I am happy to say that everyone that I have met in my life, I have gained something from them; be it negative or positive, it has enforced and reinforced my life in some aspect."
~Walter Payton

Prep TIME
I am applying this quote today by:
_____
_____
_____

I can share this quote with:
_____
_____
_____

Review TIME
I applied this quote today by:
_____
_____
_____

Moving forward I can:
_____
_____
_____

"Thousands of candles can be lighted from a single candle, and the life of that candle will not be shortened. Happiness never decreases by being shared." ~Buddha

Prep TIME
I am applying this quote today by:

_____
_____
_____

I can share this quote with:

_____
_____
_____

Review TIME
I applied this quote today by:

_____
_____
_____

Moving forward I can:

_____
_____
_____

"Our life is what our thoughts make it."
~Marcus Aurelius

Prep TIME
I am applying this quote today by:

_____
_____
_____

I can share this quote with:

_____
_____
_____

Review TIME
I applied this quote today by:

_____
_____
_____

Moving forward I can:

_____
_____
_____

"If you always put limits on everything you do, physical or anything else, it will spread into your work and into your life. There are no limits. There are only plateaus, and you must not stay there. You must go beyond them."
~Bruce Lee

Prep TIME
I am applying this quote today by:

_____
_____
_____

I can share this quote with:

_____
_____
_____

Review TIME
I applied this quote today by:

_____
_____
_____

Moving forward I can:

_____
_____
_____

"Words are powerful. They let you turn problems into challenges, challenges into opportunities, and opportunities into successes." ~Brenda Jones

Prep TIME
I am applying this quote today by:

_____
_____
_____

I can share this quote with:

_____
_____
_____

Review TIME
I applied this quote today by:

_____
_____
_____

Moving forward I can:

_____
_____
_____

"Strive not to be a success, but rather to be of value." ~Albert Einstein

Prep TIME
I am applying this quote today by:

_____
_____
_____

I can share this quote with:

_____
_____
_____

Review TIME
I applied this quote today by:

_____
_____
_____

Moving forward I can:

_____
_____
_____

"It's your outlook on life that counts. If you take yourself lightly and don't take yourself too seriously, pretty soon you can find the humor in our everyday lives. And sometimes it can be a lifesaver." ~Betty White

Prep TIME
I am applying this quote today by:

_____
_____
_____

I can share this quote with:

_____
_____
_____

Review TIME
I applied this quote today by:

_____
_____
_____

Moving forward I can:

_____
_____
_____

"Success is nothing more than a few simple disciplines, practiced every day." ~Jim Rohn

Prep TIME
I am applying this quote today by:

_____

_____

_____

I can share this quote with:

_____

_____

_____

Review TIME
I applied this quote today by:

_____

_____

_____

Moving forward I can:

_____

_____

_____

"Daring to set boundaries is about having the courage to love ourselves, even when we risk disappointing others." ~Brené Brown

Prep TIME
I am applying this quote today by:

_____
_____
_____

I can share this quote with:

_____
_____
_____

Review TIME
I applied this quote today by:

_____
_____
_____

Moving forward I can:

_____
_____
_____

"Always put your best self forward, and keep a smile on your face, because you never know when someone is being encouraged by, or falling in love with your smile."
~Kayla Moffett Stevenson

Prep TIME
I am applying this quote today by:

_____
_____
_____

I can share this quote with:

_____
_____
_____

Review TIME
I applied this quote today by:

_____
_____
_____

Moving forward I can:

_____
_____
_____

"Shallow men believe in luck. Strong men believe in cause and effect."
~Ralph Waldo Emerson

Prep TIME
I am applying this quote today by:

_____
_____
_____

I can share this quote with:

_____
_____
_____

Review TIME
I applied this quote today by:

_____
_____
_____

Moving forward I can:

_____
_____
_____

"Be thankful for what you have; you'll end up having more. If you concentrate on what you don't have, you will never, ever have enough."
~Oprah Winfrey

Prep TIME
I am applying this quote today by:

_____
_____
_____

I can share this quote with:

_____
_____
_____

Review TIME
I applied this quote today by:

_____
_____
_____

Moving forward I can:

_____
_____
_____

"I've learned that fear limits you and your vision. It serves as blinders to what may be just a few steps down the road for you. The journey is valuable, but believing in your talents, your abilities, and your self-worth can empower you to walk down an even brighter path. Transforming fear into freedom - how great is that?" ~Soledad O'Brien

Prep TIME
I am applying this quote today by:

_____
_____
_____

I can share this quote with:

_____
_____
_____

Review TIME
I applied this quote today by:

_____
_____
_____

Moving forward I can:

_____
_____
_____

"I work really hard at trying to see the big picture and not getting stuck in ego. I believe we're all put on this planet for a purpose, and we all have a different purpose... When you connect with that love and that compassion, that's when everything unfolds."
~Ellen DeGeneres

Prep TIME
I am applying this quote today by:
_____
_____
_____

I can share this quote with:
_____
_____
_____

Review TIME
I applied this quote today by:
_____
_____
_____

Moving forward I can:
_____
_____
_____

"We are what we repeatedly do. Excellence, then, is not an act but a habit." ~Aristotle

Prep TIME
I am applying this quote today by:

_____
_____
_____

I can share this quote with:

_____
_____
_____

Review TIME
I applied this quote today by:

_____
_____
_____

Moving forward I can:

_____
_____
_____

"What other people think about me is not my business." ~Michael J. Fox

Prep TIME
I am applying this quote today by:

_____
_____
_____

I can share this quote with:

_____
_____
_____

Review TIME
I applied this quote today by:

_____
_____
_____

Moving forward I can:

_____
_____
_____

"We can bring positive energy into our daily lives by smiling more, talking to strangers in line, replacing handshakes with hugs, and calling our friends just to tell them we love them." ~Brandon Jenner

Prep TIME
I am applying this quote today by:

_____
_____
_____

I can share this quote with:

_____
_____
_____

Review TIME
I applied this quote today by:

_____
_____
_____

Moving forward I can:

_____
_____
_____

"Prosperity is your ability to trust that the divine will provide and replenish."
~Glenn Morshower

Prep TIME
I am applying this quote today by:

_____
_____
_____

I can share this quote with:

_____
_____
_____

Review TIME
I applied this quote today by:

_____
_____
_____

Moving forward I can:

_____
_____
_____

Dr. Robert Jones and Brenda Jones, MA; MNLP, MHt, MTT

"Natural ability is important, but you can go far without it if you have the focus, drive, desire and positive attitude." ~Kirsten Sweetland

Prep TIME
I am applying this quote today by:

_____
_____
_____

I can share this quote with:

_____
_____
_____

Review TIME
I applied this quote today by:

_____
_____
_____

Moving forward I can:

_____
_____
_____

"I believe that you should gravitate to people who are doing productive and positive things with their lives." ~Nadia Comaneci

Prep TIME
I am applying this quote today by:

_____
_____
_____

I can share this quote with:

_____
_____
_____

Review TIME
I applied this quote today by:

_____
_____
_____

Moving forward I can:

_____
_____
_____

"There are two ways of spreading light: to be the candle or the mirror that reflects it."
~Edith Wharton

Prep TIME
I am applying this quote today by:

_____
_____
_____

I can share this quote with:

_____
_____
_____

Review TIME
I applied this quote today by:

_____
_____
_____

Moving forward I can:

_____
_____
_____

"Nothing is impossible, the word itself says 'I'm possible'!" ~Audrey Hepburn

Prep TIME
I am applying this quote today by:

_____
_____
_____

I can share this quote with:

_____
_____
_____

Review TIME
I applied this quote today by:

_____
_____
_____

Moving forward I can:

_____
_____
_____

"**Learn to enjoy every minute of your life. Be happy now. Don't wait for something outside of yourself to make you happy in the future. Think how really precious is the time you have to spend, whether it's at work or with your family. Every minute should be enjoyed and savored.**" **~Earl Nightingale**

Prep TIME
I am applying this quote today by:

_____

_____

_____

I can share this quote with:

_____

_____

_____

Review TIME
I applied this quote today by:

_____

_____

_____

Moving forward I can:

_____

_____

_____

"Learning is a process that takes a lifetime."
~Sarah Snyder

Prep TIME
I am applying this quote today by:

_____
_____
_____

I can share this quote with:

_____
_____
_____

Review TIME
I applied this quote today by:

_____
_____
_____

Moving forward I can:

_____
_____
_____

"We can learn something new anytime we believe we can." ~Virginia Satir

Prep TIME
I am applying this quote today by:

_____
_____
_____

I can share this quote with:

_____
_____
_____

Review TIME
I applied this quote today by:

_____
_____
_____

Moving forward I can:

_____
_____
_____

"Don't limit yourself. Many people limit themselves to what they think they can do. You can go as far as your mind lets you. What you believe, remember, you can achieve."
~Mary Kay Ash

Prep TIME
I am applying this quote today by:

_____
_____
_____

I can share this quote with:

_____
_____
_____

Review TIME
I applied this quote today by:

_____
_____
_____

Moving forward I can:

_____
_____
_____

"Don't aim for success if you want it; just do what you love and believe in, and it will come naturally." ~David Frost

Prep TIME
I am applying this quote today by:

_____
_____
_____

I can share this quote with:

_____
_____
_____

Review TIME
I applied this quote today by:

_____
_____
_____

Moving forward I can:

_____
_____
_____

"I do not fix problems. I fix my thinking. The problems fix themselves." ~Louise Hay

Prep TIME
I am applying this quote today by:

_____
_____
_____

I can share this quote with:

_____
_____
_____

Review TIME
I applied this quote today by:

_____
_____
_____

Moving forward I can:

_____
_____
_____

"Happiness is not something you postpone for the future; it is something you design for the present." ~Jim Rohn

Prep TIME
I am applying this quote today by:

_____
_____
_____

I can share this quote with:

_____
_____
_____

Review TIME
I applied this quote today by:

_____
_____
_____

Moving forward I can:

_____
_____
_____

"Change your thoughts and you change your world." ~Norman Vincent Peale

Prep TIME
I am applying this quote today by:

_____
_____
_____

I can share this quote with:

_____
_____
_____

Review TIME
I applied this quote today by:

_____
_____
_____

Moving forward I can:

_____
_____
_____

"Our deepest fear is not that we are inadequate. It is that we are powerful beyond our measure. It is our light, not our darkness that most frightens us. We ask ourselves, 'Who am I to be brilliant, gorgeous, talented, fabulous?' Actually, who are you not to be? Your playing small does not serve the world. There is nothing enlightened about shrinking so that other people won't feel insecure around you." ~Marianne Williamson

Prep TIME
I am applying this quote today by:

_____
_____
_____

I can share this quote with:

_____
_____
_____

Review TIME
I applied this quote today by:

_____
_____
_____

Moving forward I can:

_____
_____
_____

"I truly believe that everything that we do and everyone that we meet is put in our path for a purpose. There are no accidents; we're all teachers - if we're willing to pay attention to the lessons we learn, trust our positive instincts and not be afraid to take risks or wait for some miracle to come knocking at our door." ~Marla Gibbs

Prep TIME
I am applying this quote today by:

_____
_____
_____

I can share this quote with:

_____
_____
_____

Review TIME
I applied this quote today by:

_____
_____
_____

Moving forward I can:

_____
_____
_____

"Everything in its own time, for its own reasons... and for my best interest."
~Brenda Jones

Prep TIME
I am applying this quote today by:
_____
_____
_____

I can share this quote with:
_____
_____
_____

Review TIME
I applied this quote today by:
_____
_____
_____

Moving forward I can:
_____
_____
_____

www.ingramcontent.com/pod-product-compliance
Lightning Source LLC
Chambersburg PA
CBHW061151040426
42445CB00013B/1649